Jesus and the Meaning of Easter

Children's Christianity Books

Speedy Publishing LLC

40 E. Main St. #1156

Newark, DE 19711

www.speedypublishing.com

Copyright 2016

All Rights reserved. No part of this book may be reproduced or used in any way or form or by any means whether electronic or mechanical, this means that you cannot record or photocopy any material ideas or tips that are provided in this book

What is Easter?

Easter is the celebration of the resurrection of Jesus Christ, when he rose from the dead. He was crucified on a Friday, and rose from the dead on the third day, Sunday. Easter is usually celebrated on the first Sunday after the full moon that follows the Spring Equinox on March 21st.

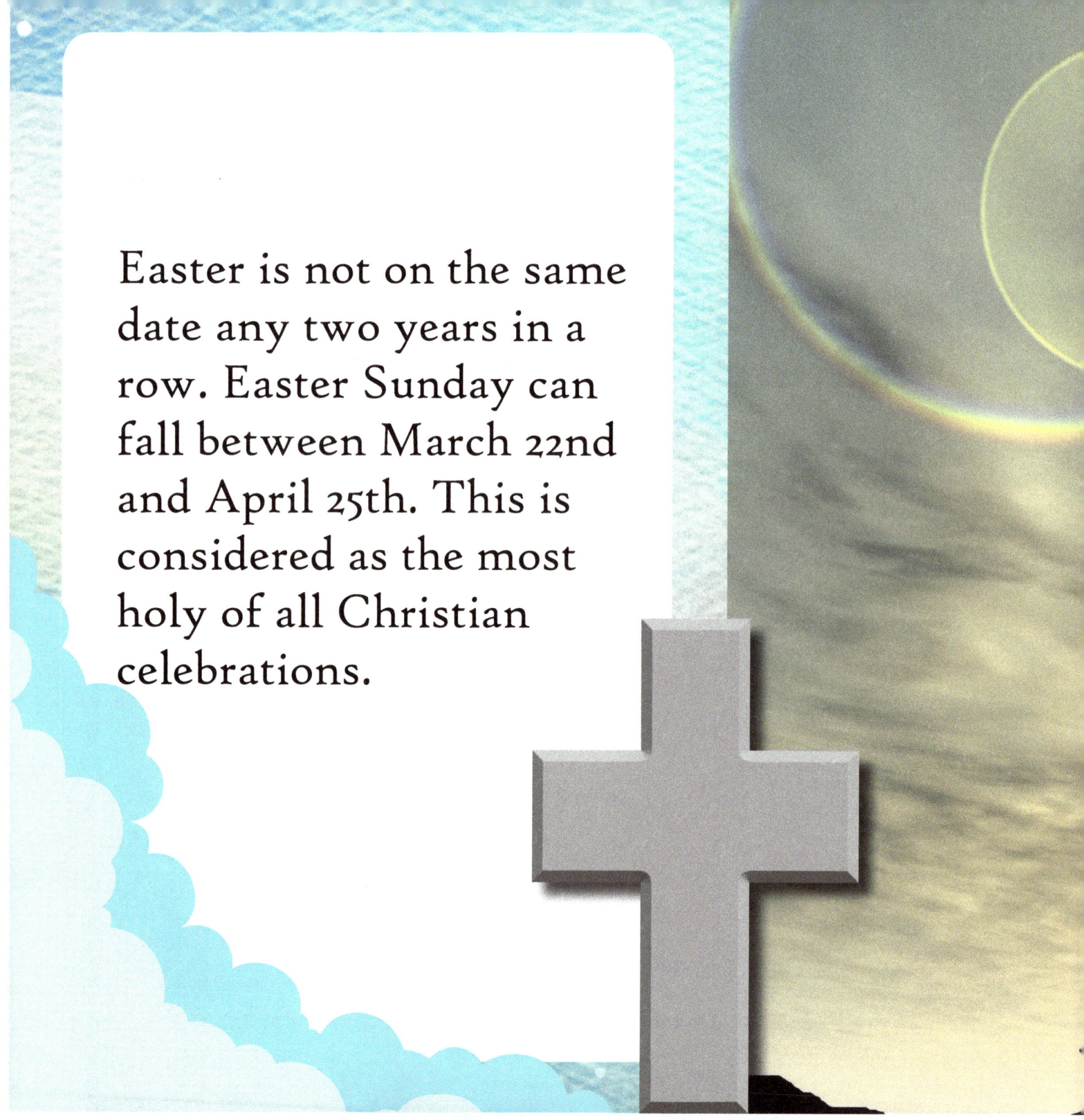

Easter is not on the same date any two years in a row. Easter Sunday can fall between March 22nd and April 25th. This is considered as the most holy of all Christian celebrations.

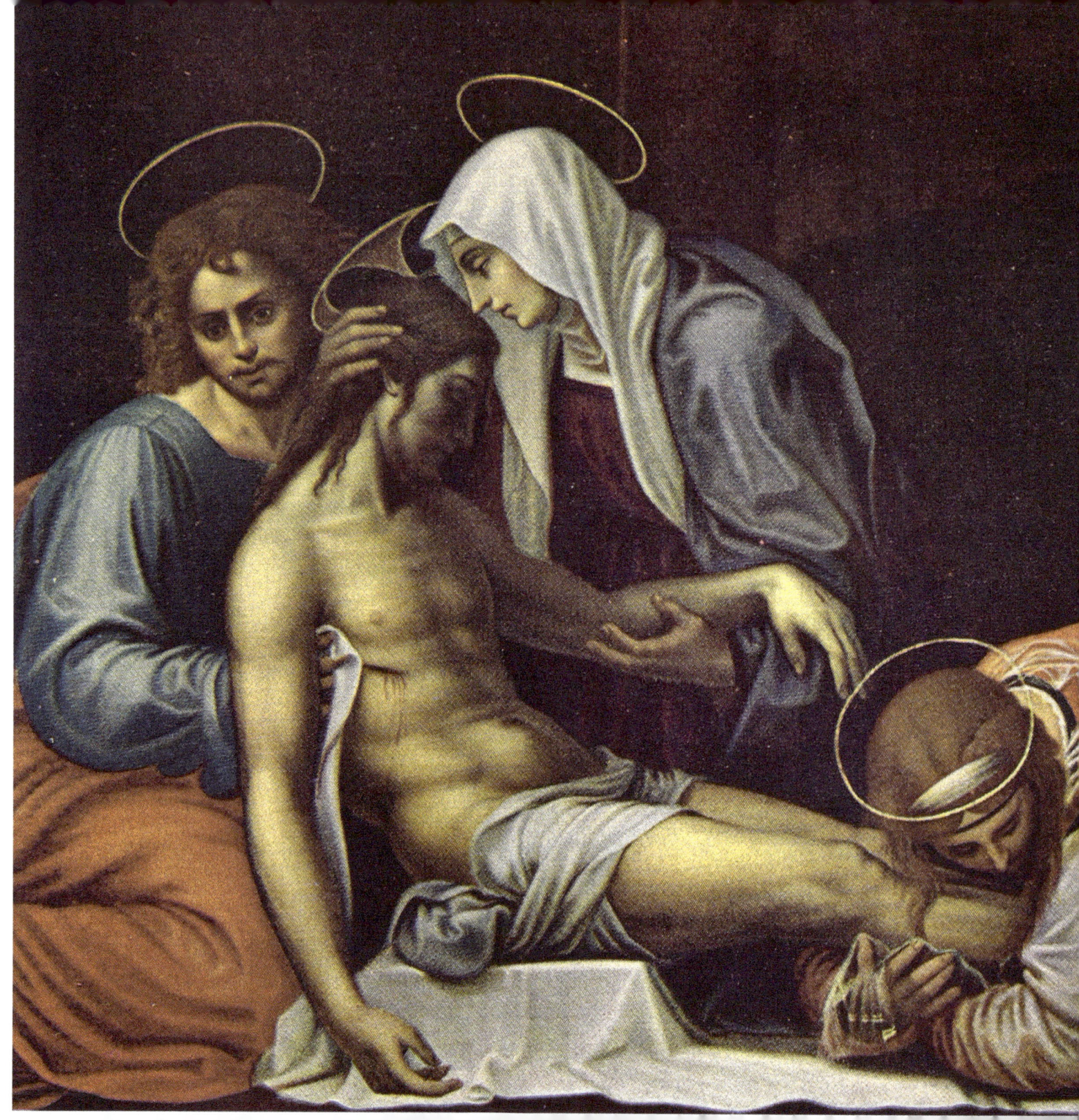

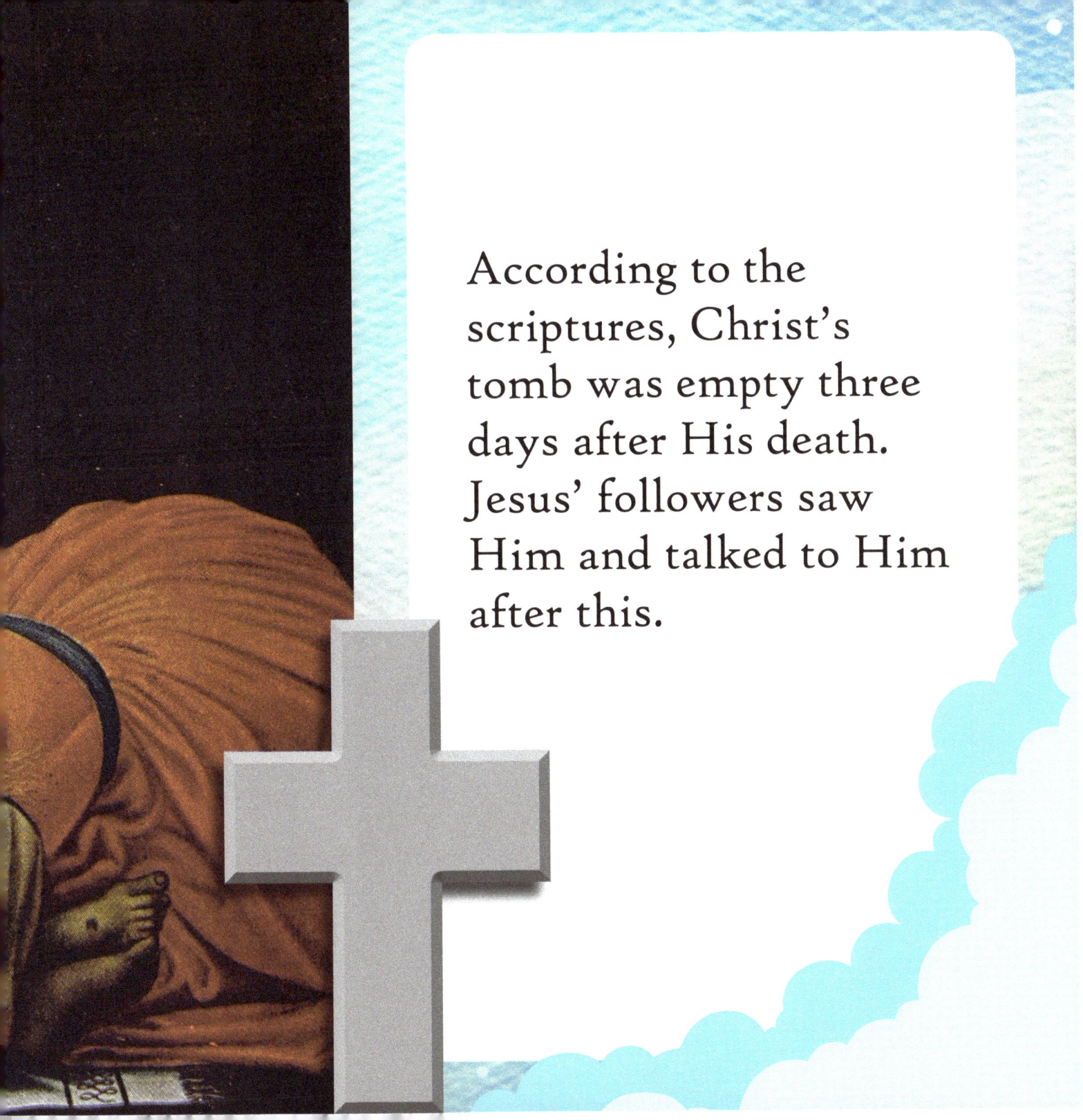

According to the scriptures, Christ's tomb was empty three days after His death. Jesus' followers saw Him and talked to Him after this.

This is why Christians believe that they have the hope of a new life, and that they can have an everlasting life in Heaven.

WHY DO WE CELEBRATE THIS?

We are all part of God's plan. He gives us life and free-will, and invites us to choose to love and obey him.

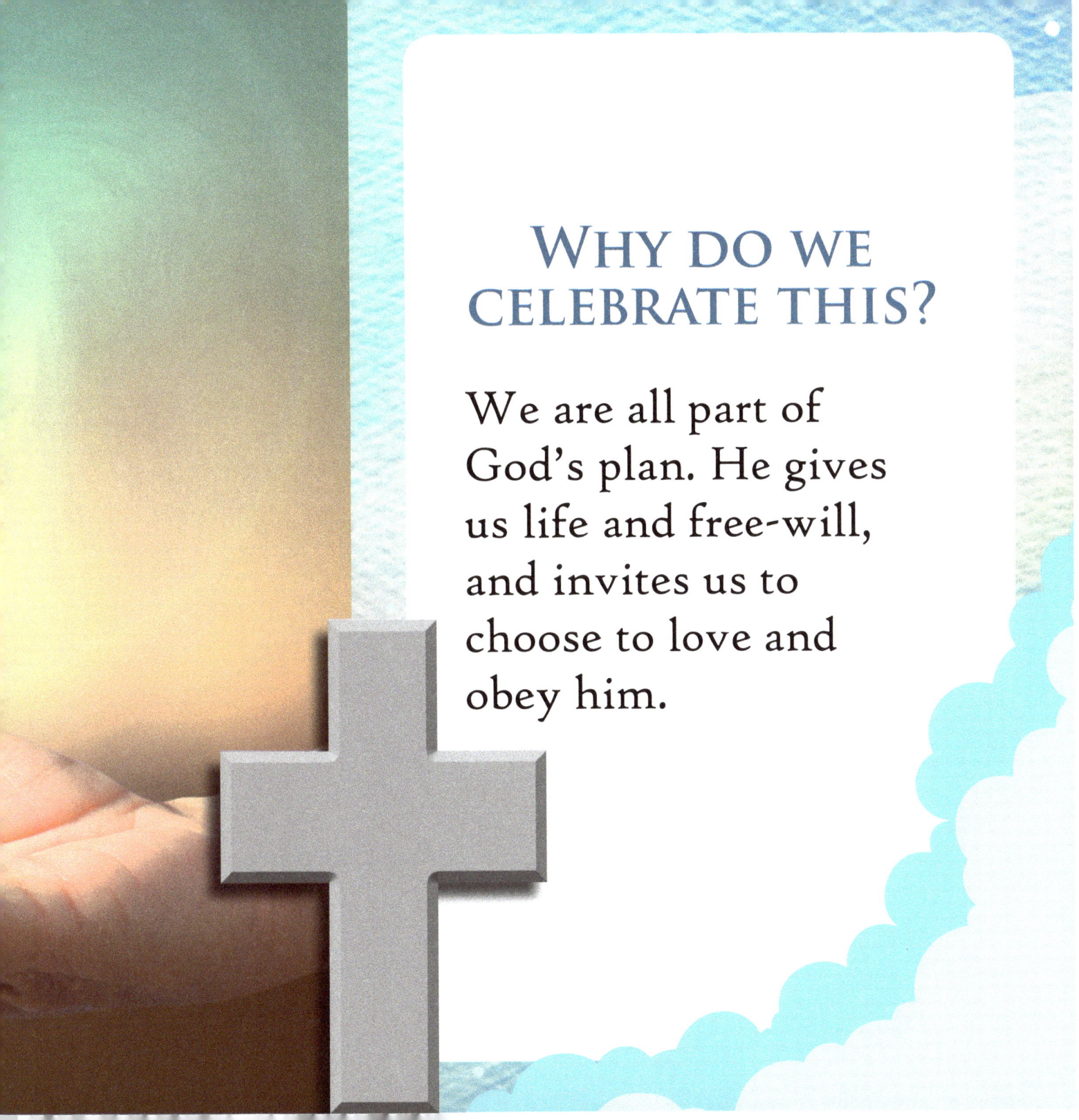

In our earthly journey, there are many temptations around us and when we give in to those temptations, we sin. When we live for sin instead of living for God, we cannot enter the kingdom of God after we die.

The first people God created were Adam and Eve. He loved them so much! They walked with Him every day in the Garden of Eden.

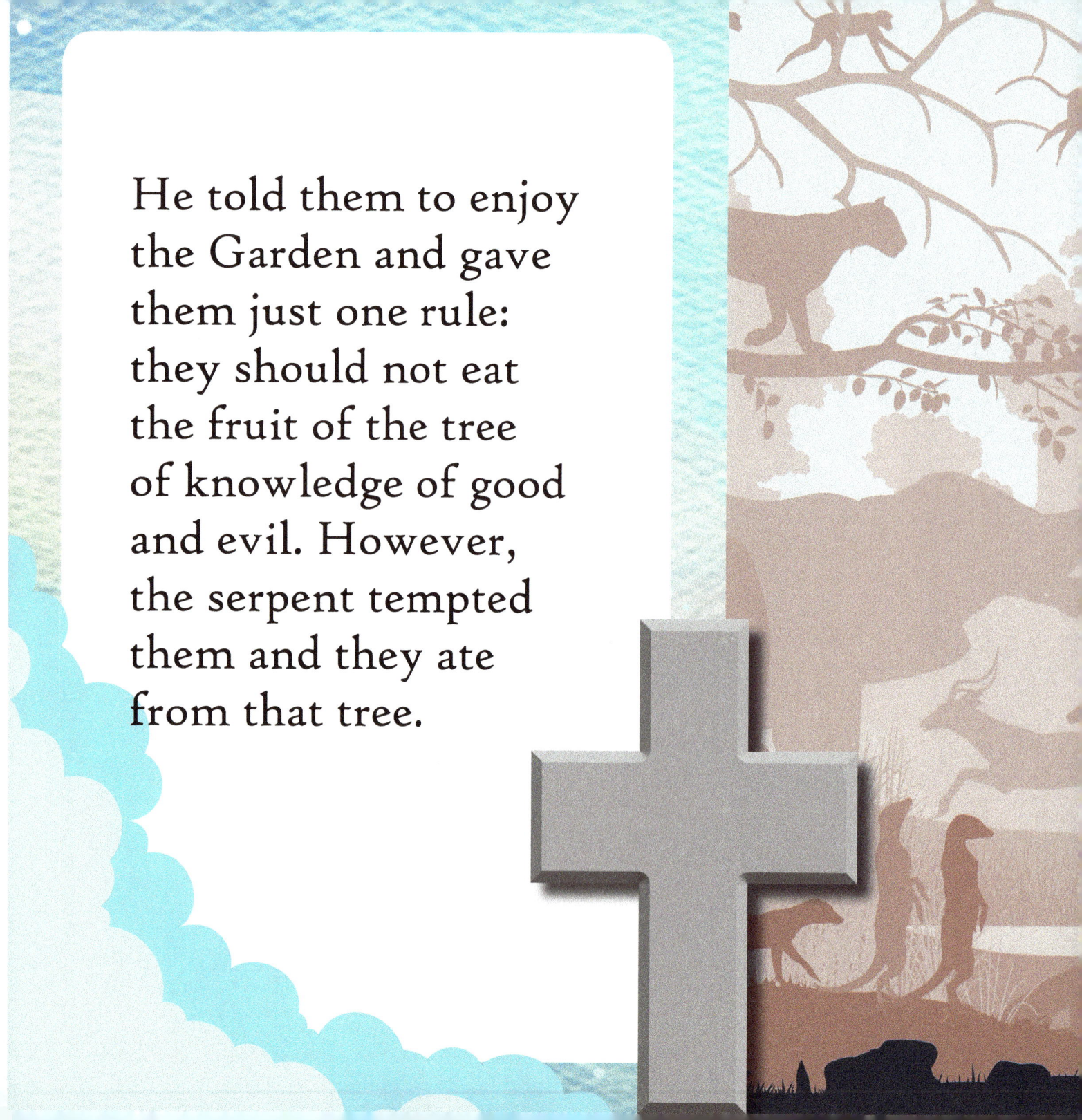

He told them to enjoy the Garden and gave them just one rule: they should not eat the fruit of the tree of knowledge of good and evil. However, the serpent tempted them and they ate from that tree.

God was very sad. He needed to cast them out of the garden because they were not yet fit to live in it. While people live for sin, they cannot walk with God.

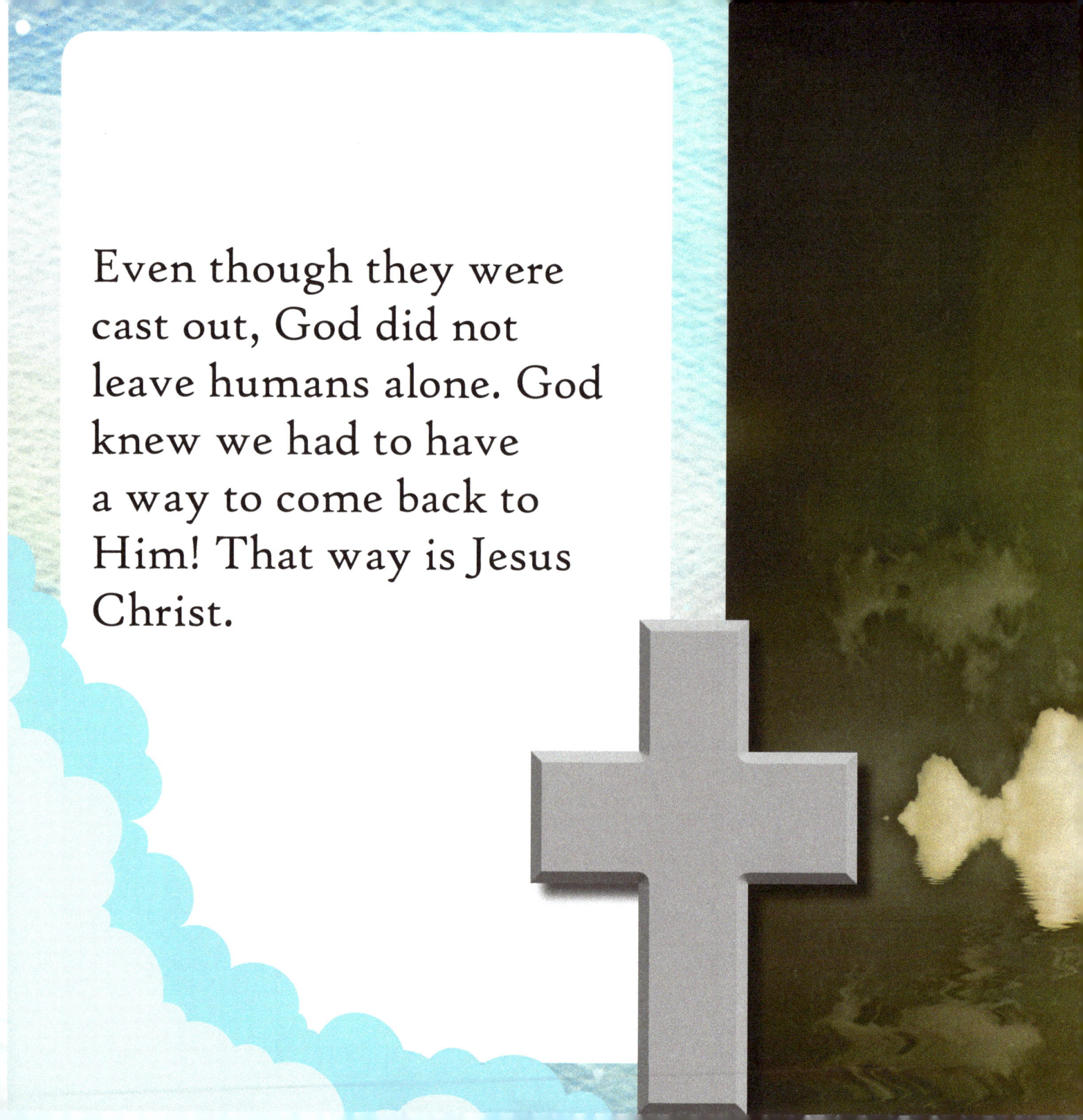

Even though they were cast out, God did not leave humans alone. God knew we had to have a way to come back to Him! That way is Jesus Christ.

God sent His very own Son to help us find our way back to Him. Jesus lived struggled, suffered, and died as a human to break the power of sin and death over us. He is called the Holy Lamb of God. Jesus was perfect and He did not sin.

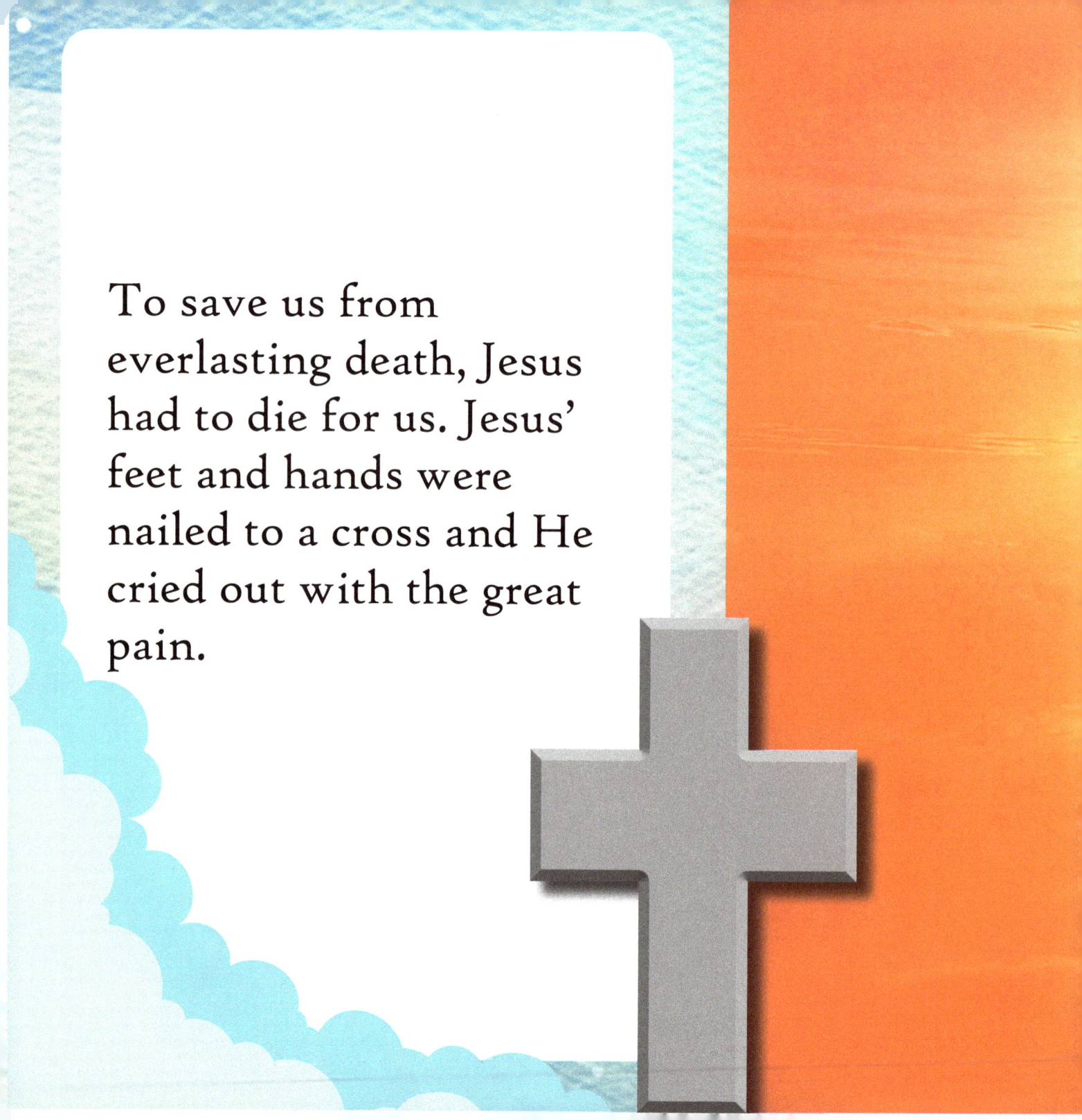

To save us from everlasting death, Jesus had to die for us. Jesus' feet and hands were nailed to a cross and He cried out with the great pain.

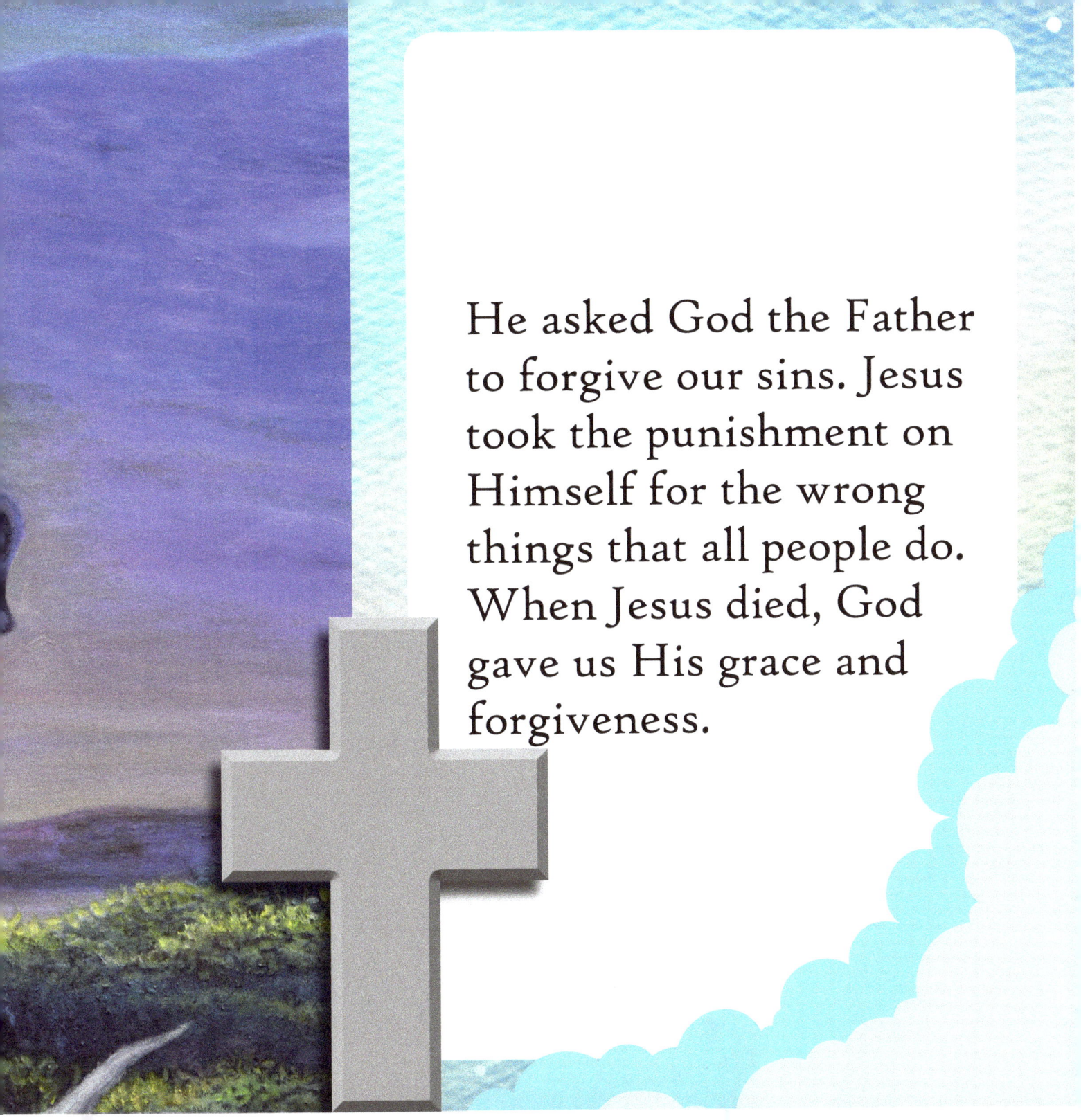

He asked God the Father to forgive our sins. Jesus took the punishment on Himself for the wrong things that all people do. When Jesus died, God gave us His grace and forgiveness.

This is not because we are good, or because we deserve it, but because of the love Jesus has for us. Christ's sacrifice gives us the gift of repentance and forgiveness.

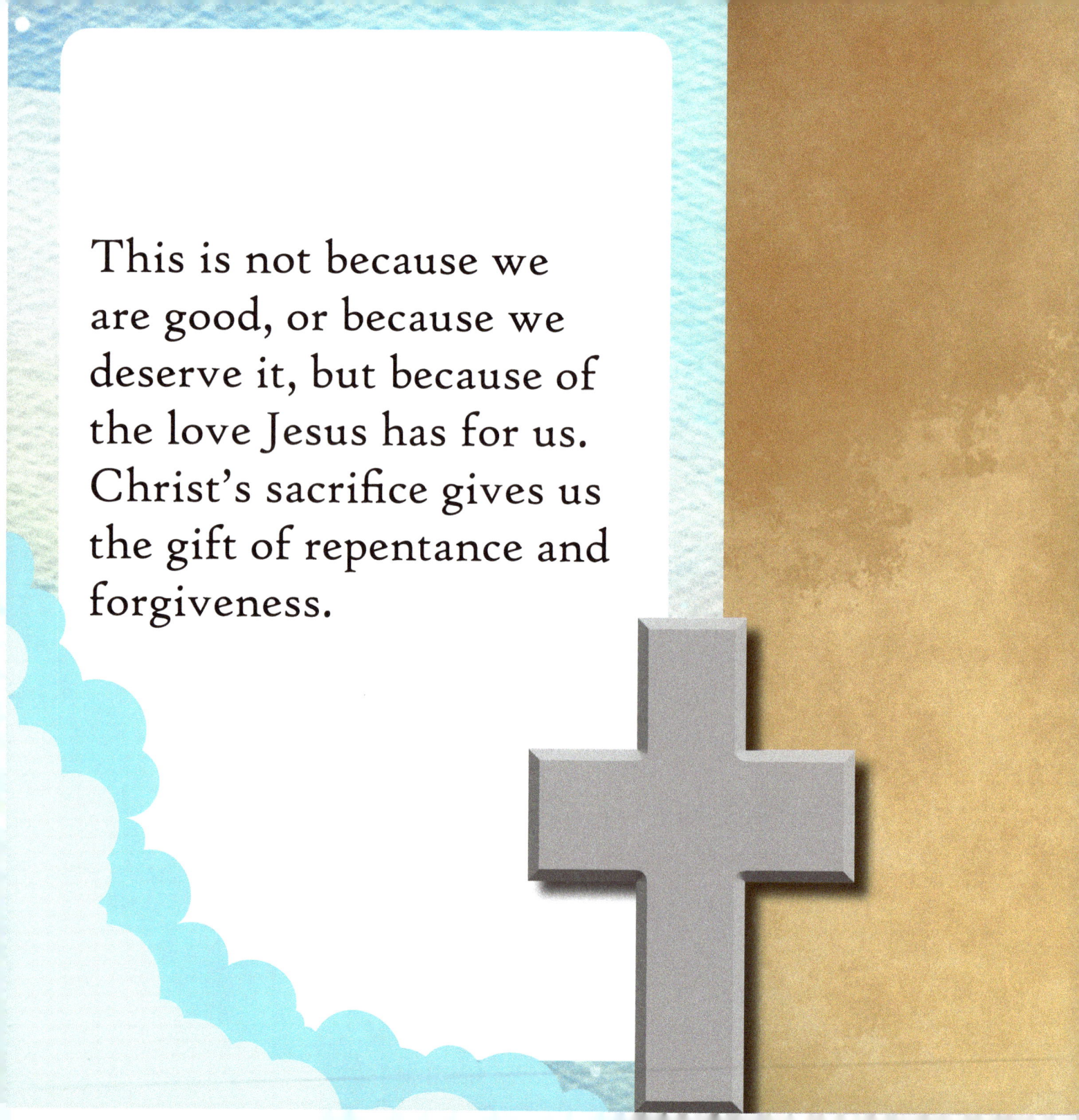

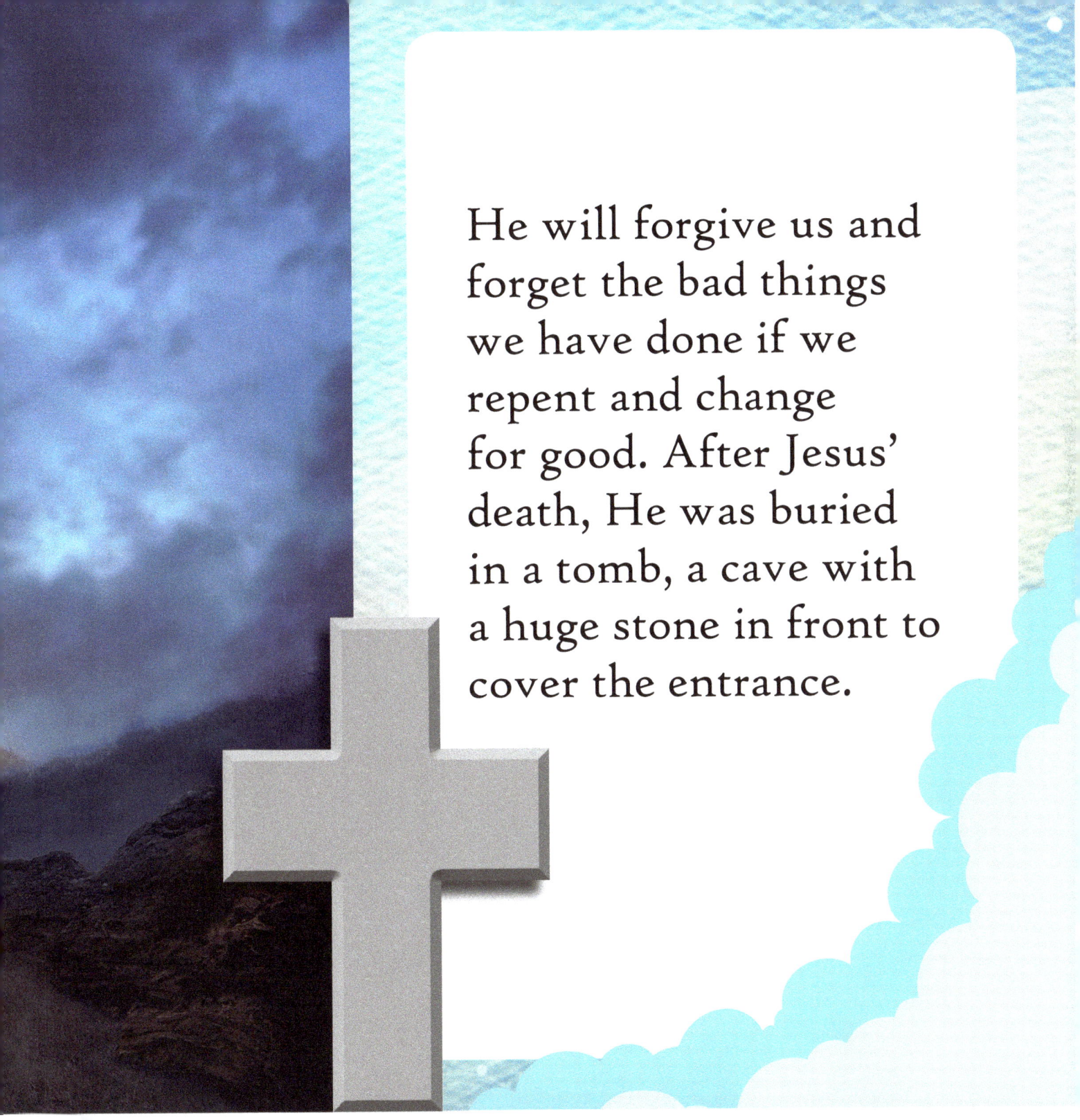

He will forgive us and forget the bad things we have done if we repent and change for good. After Jesus' death, He was buried in a tomb, a cave with a huge stone in front to cover the entrance.

On the third day, something wonderful happened. The friends of Jesus discovered the stone was rolled away and the tomb was empty. Then they saw an angel who told them what had happened. Then they said, "He is Risen!"

As a resurrected being, Jesus came to see His friends. Other people also saw that He was alive again. Jesus went back up to heaven. When He came into a new life with His Father, He gave us new life, too.

As Jesus left to go back to heaven, He asked Father God to send the Holy Spirit to be with us. The Holy Spirit lives in the hearts of God's children and He fills our empty hearts with God's love!

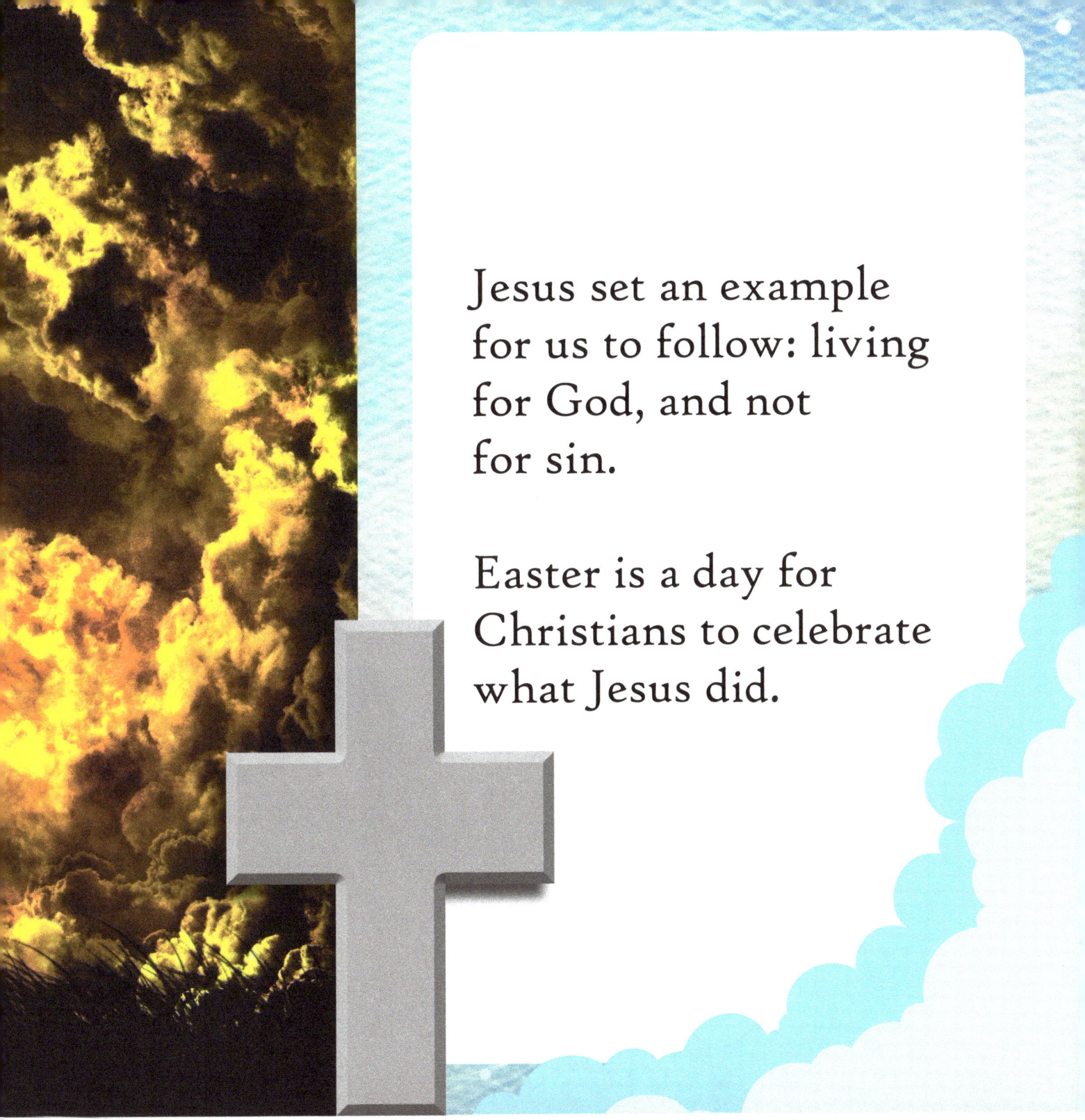

Jesus set an example for us to follow: living for God, and not for sin.

Easter is a day for Christians to celebrate what Jesus did.

CPSIA information can be obtained
at www.ICGtesting.com
Printed in the USA
BVIIW01s0731180318
510880BV00005B/109/P